Frédéric Delalot

washingtonias and zoetropes 5

KDP Editions

Dance ancient labors, the road

The arrival under the arches...

At the detachment...

We live from looks...

At random heights...

Furrows of life, ink in the air

Figures for the years...

The breathtaking beaches, summaries

Voids, wild herbs...

On the sea, some denser word

Space...

At the borders of the seconds...

Always the same dream...

They simply observe...

Out of time...

Panting, in the perfect heat

Always the same sequence...

Billions of emphases...

In hallucinogenic areas

As a result...

Coming and going...

We met her...

Like this...

Attractions and leisure...

Montreal, and length

Not everything is coherent in the moment

Small place of shows...

Getting out of the bends, ether curtain...

Facades, departure, away from the mirages

Nights passed, almost ends...

Dreams, intuitions, between cars

This part, near the Rayol...

The coves, the faces...

Sleepy villages, towards the South...

Like a flight, a bit scattered islets

Exchanged for pleasures...

All-encompassing evening, almost a hurry...

2

Dance ancient labors, the road

Unlimited minutes, serenity, horizon...

Caresses, go to the other morning...

Basically, surfing on the lines

Like wanderings...

From the present moment...

A blue ray in the evening horizon...

The century unfolding, speaking to infinity

There is a total book, a meaning under the meaning.

I remember the temptation...

To grab concerts...

Improvised, ancient labors

The road of momentum...

Intense one-second nets

Mythological of the coast...

Moors, it doesn't matter...

The arrival under the arches...

I dreamed that our names were traveling...

Evenings in a hurry from the roads, refuellers

From July, from elsewhere, walls...

Heroic victories, primitive traces.

Notes...

Repetitive...

Pretext...

To gouaches

At the detachment

From a city...

Spheres...

Old...

Thirsty...

And comfortable...

The look...

Chance of gestures

Awake, we phoenixes...

Humble fools of a story

A revival

Mountain, fortuitous revenge.

We live from looks...

Between mirrors, memories

Escape from this trot...

We know by the thousands

Devouring the peaks...

Above the statues...

Indelible moments

This impression...

Midnight...

Silence, doors ajar

Contained entire troops...

Refining, surfaces...

Indian seasons...

Alcohols, on zinc...

Skylights of our senses...

At random heights...

Along cult spaces

Under the storm of the senses...

Huge wave...

Of light opium...

Where we clung between the sails.

Billion...

Emphases

Abandonment...

Sequences...

And the time comes...

Perpetual table

In the city...

The life of clones

Escaped through the window intertwined...

And whitens the song of drunkenness...

I will identify the energetic passions

Furrows of life, ink in the air...

Dive...

Dolphins...

And enjoy the bodies...

Nirvana, since the day before.

Prime emotion...

Outside, superfluous...

May my soul love

Men saved their minds

Replaced by the desert of a garden

Facing the splendid ocean...

Figures for the years...

That I replaced...

Fountains of materials.

Clocks, a parallel universe

Encouraged her to open up...

In her youth...

During the nights...

Already, the night takes me away...

Field of possibilities...

The new city was watering us

Reflections of silver...

I had kept the imprint...

The breathtaking beaches, summaries

In the hands of carousels...

We'll see the crazy hours...

Sparkling slowness...

Fluid slammed doors

Waves, silhouettes...

Full of parallel worlds...

Light, vast impression...

So little palpable, of a space

The closing of dreams...

Not to mention the ships...

Voids, wild herbs...

In heaven, sovereign hearts...

The margin that separates us, from dawn...

Temples and tides that we imagine at night

The present moment, in the stolen words...

In the dark, the ephemeral mixes...

Engulfs images, sounds, globality...

Through blue filters, which rest us.

Near the lights...

Thinking, in addition...

I was going to get a notebook

From Frankish cities, on these lands...

On the sea, some denser word

Richer and better known future...

Free time to live...

To be quite frank

First invisible city...

Space...

History...

With regard to pioneers

Partially defined...

Maintaining the status...

Extraterrestrial, orchestrated

When I fit in...

Virtually...

Exit bias...

Innocuous...

Meetings...

Virtual regulators.

Sand made easy...

In love with artifacts...

And worlds...

Because of an illusion

Resulting from a modulation...

The ark of the world...

At the frontiers of the seconds

The clan in extenso, amaranth

First idea...

Assumptions...

Stories...

First Story

Trees, behind...

The large windows...

Absolute integrity...

And unity of the ideal time.

High constructions

The gusts bewitch

The scrolls...

Crossings

The forge...

On the street...

Always the same dream...

And their ideas intersect

In the aisles of the stadium...

With other philanthropists...

From the view of the city, beautiful

They simply observe...

Don't exist yet...

Inventors...

Finalists...

In the clearing...

Racket sport

Design...

Although philosophers

Gymnics...

With or without a ball...

And although she knew

Centuries...

At the same time...

L'Anse aux Meadows...

At the northern tip

Seven thousand years...

To the West...

Silver ink...

And alizarine...

A few hours

Characters

Gesture fluid

Or look...

Sea level...

Out of time...

There were these gems.

Millennial temple

Riders...

Mythical places...

A coincidence...

The margin of reality

And later...

I had found an open car

Panting, in the perfect heat...

American superstrings.

Joy attaches...

The triumph...

Dominating a Zen court

With long impulses...

And rechargeable, our time

Led to an extreme beach...

Always the same sequence...

Under the eternity of azure...

I prefer...

Right now...

The tunes...

Simple happiness.

Our slices of escape

As we arrive...

Towards the port, above...

Red umbrellas...

Where we clung

Between the sails...

Billions of emphases...

From a memory...

We detailed the vault...

Celestial, and the branches...

Our insomniac smiles

Flipping through an art magazine

Preamble...

Or even speed

To stroll...

Here and there...

Scrutinizing the distance

Cross-legged...

Chapters...

A little vehemence...

In hallucinogenic areas

She had a large workshop...

There, she told me about the rhythm

Many years ago...

Other levels of pleasure...

Sensation...

That I had maintained

Clearly...

Cohesion...

Motivation

Expressed...

Retirement...

Together...

Again...

As a result...

I was trying to understand

In the early morning...

What's more...

The evenings...

Magnetic...

Attracted youth

And the clothes...

As the possibilities

And a detachment...

Between two worlds...

Contemplate...

Serenely...

The hazards...

The comings and goings

In the countryside...

Season...

From tablets...

Which touched the ceiling.

Arose...

Towers...

There was Paris

We met her...

Intermittently...

Company...

Air...

Relaxation

In the trees...

When I was twenty-two years old

And she was eighteen, by car...

As far as Ampuriabrava...

Like this...

We had disembarked

Bare branches...

One-second nets...

Intense...

We had participated

Happy drills...

Discovering...

From this corner...

Location of courts

Really steamy...

Everyone was drinking...

Very stealthily...

Attractions and leisure...

From north to south...

She told me

Her history...

Wave...

Makeup...

Chance at the beginning

Pell-mell...

Observation...

Offset...

Cities and seaside

It was not nothing...

Texts that encroached

On her nights...

And universal time...

Montreal, and length

Game board...

Library...

Reading...

Hours...

Of a crazy appeasement.

Book in your pocket...

Or by hand...

Hypnotized by twentieth century

On the same colored sofa

Leading platoon of my way...

And others, in Paris, the trips...

In Meaux, as it was hot...

Not everything is coherent in the moment

Go out...

By chance...

Of course...

The socialist years.

Grisette of Montpellier...

Small place of shows

In the west, often...

The gallant Indies...

Crowd...

Friendships...

Circle...

With its smooth horses

I'm going to be a hundred years old...

There was a capital...

Vertiginous mountains

Boxes, displays

Insatiable...

Outings during the winter...

On the Plateau, full reality

Subtle links between beings...

Heterogeneous decorations, modern lines

Getting out of the bends, ether curtain

From a calming, the pace of the laps...

Later, Park Slope and spirals

Night of spaces, calls...

Going out in an era...

Of joy, a few hours

On the other side of the weekends

Building unexpectedly, bends.

Place de la Comédie, Bercy Village

Heat wave, bazaar, a plane to take

The compact crowd comes alive...

A slow canoe...

Stacks of books, bookstores...

The kilometers of covers...

Landscapes paraded, allegory ...

Facades, departure, away from the mirages

Didn't matter...

Trends rubbed shoulders, utopian

Sometimes distance, place, dock...

Group of buildings...

See the city...

The unlimited highway...

Perfume of a moment...

With a little exaggeration

Reeds of the roads...

Which bordered the rough water...

By the wind, near the ponds...

Bold roads to Spain

At night, tapas, quick flight ...

Nights passed, almost ends...

Unknown streams that began we do not know where

Philosophy of the senses, young years...

Sky at the Bastille...

Cargo, workshop, gallery...

Palais de Québec...

Coming from the sybaritic plains.

Later, wanting to dissect the mechanism

Dreams, intuitions, between cars

Parked, cross streets, adjacent ...

Freedom, the huge word of battles...

Hardly complains about material contributions

There are many parts to play...

Some were listening to downloaded music

Of sand, which dried up the nomads...

The island is revealed, reverse...

Break in Athens, a summer in Paris...
Then Carnac, approximate exits
Mixtures of genres, a free house...
Playing systematically, there...

A fast boat, the waves...
Disembarking in a restaurant...
Sanctuary of laps, a slow day
Imbued with horizons...

This part, near the Rayol...
And Saint-Clair, on the wet sand...
From the beach, turrets, transcendence
Outside, it was the lack that wrote.

Which imposed its rhythm

Its caches...

Until the countryside...

Perfect curves...

Fugitive afternoon, a coffee in Castellane

And, often, going from one house to another

Attraction to the outside, between branches

Trees, sometimes imposing, stranded...

Join this mirage...

The coves, the faces...

Invaded from the South, by bike...

Large walls, cherry trees

Described wide circles...

Opulence at the passage of the streets...

Docks, ecstasy, depths

Landscapes, for a moment.

Dive back into yourself...

Looking for a title to these portions...

Like a float that was self-evident

At the end of the street...

Half lit...

From continents to osmosis

Sleepy villages, towards the South...

There are areas of transparency...

Perfect wandering that prolongs the night.

Postcard, take advantage of a post office...

Which does not exist, feel the invisible...

Like a flight, a bit scattered islands...

Indistinct nomads blending into a mirage

Further on, the implausible horizons

Which were marinating, victories of silence...

After the hours, variations...

Which sleep, sometimes, in finer orders

Time from elsewhere...

I remembered...

Flawless consistency...

The utopia of great marches.

Long place of moments...

Exchanged for pleasures...

Like the blur, the world dissipates

Sculptures differ from this world

Because there is this time, fascination

Or flight of birds, unfolding...

Inaccessible, exact infinite...

Great present moment...

Amazing entertainment...

Logic illuminates the cliffs

The long glass curves...

And the roads, the blotter of the spheres

Megacities...

Thinking about the focus, the borders

The light creates a sanctuary...

Going back to the distance...

Virgin and prehistoric territory...

The cars stop, on the ground...

Without more oil, for a time

All-encompassing evening, almost a hurry

Leaves twirled...

Drunkenness, satiated mornings...

We had surrendered

Beyond friendship...

Glare...

Granite avenues...

Pebble beach...

On the edge of the English Channel

Unforgettable refrains...

Downtown clothing...

From Montreal to Paris...

For a few hours, sauterie

End of year...

A penumbra...

The way he had...

To accompany my nights

Words, detours, chances...

She painted...

The workshop was on the top floor...

Quite protected and quiet area...

In the space we had reintegrated

Zigzagging journey...

Caravan of vehicles...

Generations of beings...

In symbiosis with nature

Outings to La Loco, Balajo...

At the Foufounes Électriques...

The impression of a new beginning

Turns by car...

We inhabited other worlds

Long on beaches...

In North America...

On the East Coast...

15

Quarter made of carelessness

Art and science...

Space-time...

Under the branches...

Century-old trees

In the evening...

Dancing, drift bar...

The times, the places...

Which were loaded with hope.

Shorts in the middle of winter...

The eve of Boxing Day

Unique sky, this café...

Which never closed...

Another world was fading away

Variable at leisure, and built...

Near a new age...

The night saw us drunk...

Live the moment, exhaust the evenings

Because we would be old, in the end...

Chalk on one of the tables...

Eliminated armchairs, comfortable...

Globality that gave everything...

Zen garden upstairs...

Vaguely bright pool

Strong warmth and crush

In Paris, the desires...

Seasonal proposals...

Let things be perfect

Immutable...

Let yourself be invaded by a gesture

For a moment...

Protest manifest, far away...

Between two books...

Being at an outpost...

Bends of the Clape...

Thin strip of sand...

Of these intense emotions.

16

Discreetly approaching an autumnal air

Sand, sea view, for a few hours

Metamorphoses, skyscrapers stood out

Dream of smooth legs

She could have been there...

Like this...

Discovery, free...

Balance had its source

In the nuances...

Red lights coming out of the sidewalks...

From the neighborhood, and during this time I saw her

Exterior of a building, between clubs and tastes

Attractions, in the night, covered with sand

She had been lying down...

Hair undone...

Pearl necklace...

We had put away the tennis balls

By chance...

Unexpectedly...

Behind a tree of the square

In psychedelic dress...

On the quiet street...

Surrounded by villas...

Panoramic...

This same presence

Finished installing the stage

By the park, in the evening...

Hypnotized us...

Leagues away...

Climbed the slopes...

Hugging us towards the shore

Brought our bodies closer together...

In order to conquer the tracks...

Sinuous, red umbrellas

Tables, wanderings...

Preserved me...

Untied space...

17

Memories of happiness

Anachronistic, peripheries

The fall of the boats, docile

The beams swept across the sky

Drunkenness, forever...

From the depths of the exciting ages...

After a sequel

Close to beaches

Waves...

Later, I looked at her body...

Lots of movies, wonders

The orange colors, and the choices...

Appeared tans, dances...

Were spinning in the street...

From Square-Dorchester...

Raspberries from other gardens

In the years, scattered words

On the top floor

I was watching...

A swimming pool...

Light...

The evening would be ours...

Forever, whatever we do

Never tired of caressing each other...

By the frost place...

Glows, orange sphere...

At the window, the branches

Back to Bastille...

Memories of months...

I remembered one summer...

There would be only memories left

From a slow, curious world...

Perfume of the unknown...

Full lightness...

The energy of exchanges

Appointment-specific

The crew of the moment.

18

And we woke up

Moisture of a new climate

Walls of the old town...

Grains of ancient power

A je ne sais quoi of fuchsia...

She didn't keep anything...

It was seeing plants...

Suspended in bubbles

Dense charm...

Music of Cape Town...

Late...

At Le Lavandou...

I could see the waves

Of Saint-Pierre-la-Mer, kitesurfing...

Then the Grau de Pissevaches, a sign...

Fluid fabrics, believing in happiness, smiling...

Sunny birthdays, the Coast of Excesses

Distant embraces, at dawn...

Flying away, the blurred photograph...

From a story, after years...

Minimal messages of attentions.

Finding yourself, after the drought...

From the summer, see her smile again...

Tropical festivals, appeared suddenly

Take a plane and find her...

New Wave places...

Whirling, on the street...

Carpet of wet leaves

Camouflage of time...

Away from the centuries

Evenings...

Like stories

Fictional representation

Asleep...

It had been lively...

And intense...

Eternity of youth.

19

Faces...

In the early afternoon

Nights...

I was following the course of things...

Really, I liked watching them

Go fast, perfect their designs...

On the fine and sensual sand...

I saw distant landscapes

In the light of spring...

Greek nights, on a lost island...

German nights...

Probable happiness, third millennium

Fast ships, like in a movie...

Which would have taken place...

In bibliolubes...

Holed up in glaciers

New dimension...

The black trees accompanied her...

With imaginary rafts...

Drought, when we walked

On the yellowed grass of the park...

In search of parties...

And discoveries...

Billions of years...

Evaporation of everything

Dream place...

We are double...

We were looking for relief

Ways to enjoy the moment...

Research, wanderings...

The powerful form of departures...

Jerky tales of our routines...

Glasses of gin-coca, caresses

Waiting for this story...

To maintain a general sense

At our construction...

In a land called fantasy...

20

Flood of worlds, before our prehistory

Maybe away from the unreasons...

Door of creative intentions...

This chance would mean travel...

First time, night of spaces...

Call, go out in an era

Getting some fresh air for years...

Indefinite noise, wavelength...

Century-old hedges, where they guessed.

Near the equator

About ten seconds...

Or even one to two minutes

Compare speeds...

During the docile night

The pleasure was eternal...

Bewitching...

The square was crowded...

Illusions, movement...

From a hair...

Thousands of worlds...

Crossed paths briefly.

And I remember the thread of the night

From the caress of the shadows, apart...

Beautiful, like a perfume...

Distant roads...

We ate blackberries...

Wild, the present carried...

Its immense sails, its multitude

Attractions, paths...

In tiny headphones...

Translucent, I listened to Bon Jovi

Snow would cover the parks...

Next to a people who were coming out...

Driving cars in how many parties

Bastille, a few hours...

I loved all those moments, the exhilaration...

Outside the world, colorful autumns...